Cover – The patchwork of fields on the Canterbury Plains, with the snow-capped Southern Alps behind. (Andris Apse)

Front endpapers – Queen Charlotte Sound, part of the Marlborough Sounds, near Picton. (Andris Apse)

Previous page – Looking up the North Taranaki coastline from the White Cliffs walkway at Tongaporutu. (P. Morath)

Opposite – A South Canterbury sheep station. (Andris Apse)

Overleaf – Sunset at Doubtful Sound in Fiordland National Park. (Andris Apse)

ISBN 1-86958-137-7

Published in 1995 by Hodder Moa Beckett Publishers Limited
[a member of the Hodder Headline Group]
28 Poland Road, Glenfield, Auckland, New Zealand

Printed through Bookbuilders, Hong Kong

NEW ZEALAND

SCENIC WONDERLAND

HODDER MOA BECKETT

NEW ZEALAND

SCENIC WONDERLAND

New Zealand's spectacular landscape makes it a very special place. Its beauties stretch from the golden sands and deep blue waters of the north to the snow-capped mountain ranges and wilderness areas of the south.

Apart from incredible beauty, the landscape also encompasses some unique features. The geysers and boiling mud pools of the Rotorua thermal region, the mystery of the Waitomo Caves, the awesome icy paths of the Fox and Franz Josef Glaciers and the incredible leaps of the Sutherland Falls.

However, it is often the "ordinary" that seems most extraordinary in travellers' eyes – an empty beach gilded by the setting sun, a perfect reflection of mountains caught in the still waters of a lake, the play of light on rolling hills or a clear stream rushing through virgin bush.

The sheer expansiveness of the landscape is often one of its overwhelming features – wonderful panoramas stretching as far as the eye can see, unfettered by the clutter of urban life.

All these features contribute to make New Zealand's landscape unique, and capture the essence of what makes the country so special.

The sun breaks through low cloud off Cape Reinga, Northland. (Andris Apse)

Previous spread: Surf rolls into the arc of the bay at Cape Maria van Diemen, Northland. (Andris Apse)

The corrugated patterns of sand dunes near Te Paki Stream at the northern end of Ninety Mile Beach. (Andris Apse)

R olling green farmland surrounding the Bay of Islands, with Kerikeri Inlet and Purerua Peninsula in the background. (Andris Apse)

Overleaf: Rangitoto Island at sunrise, surrounded by the waters of the Waitemata Harbour, Auckland. (Ian Hutcheson, Focus NZ)

Previous spread: Giant kauri trees form a soaring canopy over nikau palms and bush on the Coromandel Peninsula. (Andris Apse)

Sunrise paints the sand of Brophys Beach and the waters of Mercury Bay, on the Coromandel Peninsula. (Andris Apse)

S talactites form a fringe on the roof of Ruakuri Cave at Waitomo. (In Stock NZ)

T he Emerald Lakes, on the slopes of Mt Tongariro, in the Tongariro National Park.
(Georg Ludwig, Focus NZ)

Pohutu Geyser in full force, at Whakarewarewa, Rotorua. (Brian Enting, Keylight)

The bubbling, steaming waters of the Champagne Pool at Waiotapu. (Brian Moorehead, Focus NZ)

A fisherman tries his luck at the Waitahanui River mouth on Lake Taupo. (Andris Apse)

Overleaf: The three mountains of the volcanic plateau – Ruapehu (left), Ngauruhoe and Tongariro – with Mt Taranaki in the distance at right. (DAC)

Gannets find the perfect nesting spot on the promontory of Cape Kidnappers, Hawke's Bay. (P. Morath)

Overleaf: One of New Zealand's many beautiful waterfalls – at Waihi Falls Scenic Reserve, Hawke's Bay. (Andris Apse)

The perfect cone of Mt Taranaki, or Mt Egmont, breaks through a veil of mist. (DAC)

R ock formations rise like a huge cathedral
organ along the coast at Palliser Bay.
(Andris Apse)

Overleaf: A dolphin leaps out of the water off the
Kaikoura Coast. (Dennis Buurman, Focus NZ)

A fan of spray is forced up through the blowholes at Punakaiki, north of Greymouth, famous for its rocks shaped like stacks of pancakes.

(Jack Sprosen, Focus NZ)

Above: The Southern Alps and Fox Glacier meet farmland and native bush. (Andris Apse)

S kiers climb up to the Governors Col, with the Upper Fox Glacier in the background.
(Andris Apse)

A Squirrel helicopter flies over the Fox Glacier at sunset. (Andris Apse)

Lyttelton Harbour sheltered by surrounding hills, with Quail Island in the centre. (Andris Apse)

The wonderful tapestry of the Canterbury Plains, fringed by the Southern Alps.
(Andris Apse)

Lake Marymere, cradled in the hills of Canterbury, with the Torlesse Range in the background. (Andris Apse)

Previous spread: Rolling hills as far as the eye can see – looking south-east from Mt Studholme Station, South Canterbury. (Andris Apse)

L ake Hayes in the still of autumn, with vineyards in the foreground. (Andris Apse)

Previous spread: A bird's eye view of Queenstown from above the Skyline Restaurant, with the township on the shores of Lake Wakatipu framed by the Remarkables mountain range. (Andris Apse)

L*ady of the Sounds* cruising past a snow-dusted Mitre Peak on Milford Sound, Fiordland National Park. (Andris Apse)

The Sutherland Falls spill from Lake Quill in three giant leaps, in the Fiordland National Park. (Andris Apse)

Overleaf: Pristine beauty of the Upper Freeman Burn River passing through native forest in the Fiordland National Park. (Andris Apse)

T he golden arc of Mason Bay on Stewart Island.
(Andris Apse)

Overleaf: A pod of orcas off the Kaikoura Coast.
(Dennis Buurman, Focus NZ)

Back endpapers: The still waters of Okarito Lagoon
reflect the Southern Alps. (Andris Apse)